WEST COUNTRY TEA RECIPES

Elizabeth Hardy

DOMINO BOOKS (WALES) LTD

METRIC/IMPERIAL/AMERICAN UNITS

We are all used to doubling or halving a recipe. Thus, a Victoria sandwich may be made using 4 oz each of flour, sugar and butter with 2 eggs or 6 oz each of flour, sugar and butter with 3 eggs. The proportions of the ingredients are unchanged. This must be so for all units. Use either the metric units or the imperial units given in the recipes, do not mix the two.

It is not practical to give the exact equivalents of metric and imperial units because 1 oz equals 28.35 gm and 1 pint equals 568 ml. The tables on page vi indicate suitable quantities but liquids should be carefully added to obtain the correct consistency. See also the charts on page iv.

PINTS TO MILLILITRES AND LITRES
The following are approximations only

¼ pint = 150 ml

½ pint = 275 ml

¾ pint = 425 ml

1 pint = 575 ml

1¾ pints = 1000 ml (1 litre)

3 pints = 1½ litres

CONTENTS

© D C P and E J P, 1993.
Cover photograph by Jonathan Tew
Illustrations by Allison Fewtrell

ISBN 1 85772 055 5
Typeset by Domino Books (Wales) Ltd
Printed in Hong Kong

The following charts give the approximate equivalents for metric and imperial weights, and oven temperatures.

Ounces	Approx gm to nearest whole number	Approx gm to nearest whole 25 gm
1	28	25
2	57	50
3	85	75
4	113	125
5	142	150
6	170	175
7	198	200
8	226	225
9	255	250
10	283	275
11	311	300
12	340	350
13	368	375
14	396	400
15	428	425
16	456	450

OVEN TEMPERATURE GUIDE

	Electricity		Gas Mark
	°C	°F	
Very cool	110	225	$\frac{1}{4}$
	130	250	$\frac{1}{2}$
Cool	140	275	1
	150	300	2
Moderate	170	325	3
	180	350	4
Moderately hot	190	375	5
	200	400	6
Hot	220	425	7
	230	450	8
Very hot	240	475	9

When using this chart for weights over 16 ounces, add the appropriate figures in the column giving the nearest whole number of grammes and then adjust to the nearest unit of 25. For example, 18 oz (16 oz + 2 oz) becomes 456 + 57 = 513 to the nearest whole number and 500 gm to the nearest unit of 25.

Throughout the book, 1 teaspoon = 5 ml and 1 tablespoon = 15 ml.

FOREWORD

Teatime in the West Country is an occasion to remember. The traditional cream tea of scones, conserves, strawberries and clotted cream can be enjoyed in smart hotels, in friendly restaurants and pavement cafés, in picturesque gardens or by flickering firelight in the cool of late afternoon. Besides elegant afternoon tea, there is the more substantial 'high tea'. Intended for more hearty appetites this may include Cornish pasties, savoury dishes, sandwiches, toasted teacakes and Bath buns. Taken late in the afternoon it may replace dinner leaving the evening free until supper time.

Teatime and a cup of tea are part of the British way of life and whether you wish to prepare a light tea or a more substantial meal, this book provides some ideas and recipes which I hope will please you, your family and your friends.

Other books from the same publishers with more West Country recipes include *West Country Cooking* and *Customs and Cooking from the West Country*.

E H

AMERICAN MEASURES

American measures are given by volume and weight using standard cups and spoons.

US Standard Measuring Spoons and Cups

1 tablespoon = 3 teaspoons = ½ fluid ounce = 14.2 ml
2 tablespoons = 1 fluid ounce = 28 ml
4 tablespoons = ¼ cup
5 tablespoons = ⅓ cup
8 tablespoons = ½ cup
10 tablespoons = ⅝ cup (i.e. ⅔ approx.)
12 tablespoons = ¾ cup
16 tablespoons = 2 cups = 8 fluid ounces = ½ US pint
32 tablespoons = 2 cups = 16 fluid ounces = 1 US pint.

Metric (Imperial)	American
1 teaspoon	1 teaspoon
1 tablespoon	1 tablespoon
1½ teaspoons	2 tablespoons
2 tablespoons	3 tablespoons
3 tablespoons	¼ (scant) cup
4 tablespoons	5 tablespoons
5 tablespoons	6 tablespoons
5½ tablespoons	7 tablespoons
6 tablespoons (scant ¼ pint)	½ cup
¼ pint	⅔ cup
scant ½ pint	1 cup
½ pint (10 fl oz)	1¼ cups
¾ pint (15 fl oz)	scant 2 cups
⅘ pint (16 fl oz)	2 cups (1 pint)
1 pint (20 fl oz)	2½ cups

Metric (Imperial)	American
flour, plain or self-raising	
15 gm (½ oz)	2 tablespoons
25 gm (1 oz)	1¼ cup
100/125 gm (4 oz)	1 cup
sugar, caster or granulated, brown (firmly packed)	
15 gm (1 oz)	2 tablespoons
100/125 gm (4 oz)	½ cup
200/225 gm (8 oz)	1 cup
butter, margarine, fat	
1 oz	2 tablespoons
225 gm (8 oz)	1 cup
150 gm (5 oz) shredded suet	1 cup

1 cup (American) contains approximately

100/125 gm (4 oz) grated cheese, 50 gm (2 oz) fresh breadcrumbs, 100 gm (4 oz) dried breadcrumbs,
100/125 gm (4 oz) pickled beetroot, button mushrooms, shelled peas, red/blackcurrants, 5 oz strawberries,
175 gm (6 oz) raisins, currants, sultanas, chopped candied peel, stoned dates,
225 gm (8 oz) glacé cherries, 150 gm (5 oz) shelled whole walnuts, 100 gm (4 oz) chopped nuts,
75 gm (3 oz) dessicated coconut,
225 gm (8 oz) cottage cheese,
100/125 gm (4 oz) curry powder,
225 gm (8 oz) minced raw meat,
⅜ pint (7½ fl oz) cream.

CAKES

STRAWBERRY CREAM CAKE

METRIC	IMPERIAL
150 g self raising flour	*6 oz self raising flour*
150 g caster sugar	*6 oz caster sugar*
3 eggs	*3 eggs*
400 g strawberries	*1 lb strawberries*
450 ml cream	*¾ pint cream*

Beat the eggs and sugar until thick and creamy. Sift the flour twice. Fold the flour into the egg and sugar mixture. Grease and flour a 20 cm (8 inch) cake tin. Turn the cake mixture into the tin and bake for 35 - 40 minutes in a moderately hot oven (190°C, 375°F, gas mark 5) until the cake springs back when touched. Turn on to a wire rack to cool. Cut into three layers. Wash and hull the strawberries. Mash half the strawberries using a fork, adding a little sugar if necessary. Whip the cream. Sandwich the layers of cake with the mashed strawberries and cream. Decorate the top of the cake with cream and whole strawberries.

STRAWBERRY SHORTCAKE

METRIC	IMPERIAL
200 g plain flour	8 oz plain flour
2½ teaspoons baking powder	2½ teaspoons baking powder
½ teaspoon salt	½ teaspoon salt
75 g butter	3 oz butter
200 g caster sugar	8 oz caster sugar
125 ml milk	½ pint milk
1 egg	1 egg
400 g strawberries	1 lb strawberries

Sift the flour, baking powder and salt together. Cream the butter and sugar until soft and fluffy. Beat the egg and beat into the butter mixture. Fold in the flour mixture and add the milk. Turn into two greased 20 cm (8 inch) sandwich tins and bake in a moderately hot oven (190ºC 375ºF, gas mark 5) for 25 minutes.

Hull and wash the strawberries. Mash half of the fruit with a fork and sprinkle with caster sugar if necessary. When the cakes are cool, sandwich together with the mashed strawberries. Decorate with whipped cream and whole strawberries.

COCONUT CAKE

METRIC	IMPERIAL
200 g self raising flour	8 oz self raising flour
100 g desiccated coconut	4 oz desiccated coconut
125 g butter	5 oz butter
125 g caster sugar	5 oz caster sugar
3 eggs	3 eggs
3 tablespoons milk	3 tablespoons milk

Cream the butter and sugar together until light and fluffy. Beat the eggs one at a time and beat into the butter mixture. Mix the flour and coconut together and fold into the mixture. Add enough milk to give a dropping consistency. Grease and line a 20 cm (8 inch) cake tin with greased greaseproof paper. Turn the cake mixture into the tin and bake in a moderate oven (180°C, 350°F, gas mark 4) for one to one and a quarter hours until the cake is cooked. (A clean knife inserted into the cake should not show any trace of moist cake when withdrawn.)

WEST COUNTRY FRUIT CAKE

METRIC	IMPERIAL
400 g plain flour	1 lb plain flour
150 g butter	6 oz butter
200 g soft brown sugar	8 oz soft brown sugar
200 g mixed fruit (currants and sultanas)	8 oz mixed fruit (currants and sultanas)
1 egg	1 egg
250 ml milk	½ pint milk
2 teaspoons mixed spice	2 teaspoons mixed spice
1 teaspoon bicarbonate of soda	1 teaspoon bicarbonate of soda

Sift the flour, mixed spice and bicarbonate of soda together. Rub in the butter until the mixture looks like breadcrumbs. Stir in the sugar and fruit. Beat the egg and milk together. Make a well in the middle of the dry ingredients and pour some of the egg and milk into this. Beat and mix well. Add enough liquid to give a soft dropping consistency. Add more milk if necessary. Grease and line a 20 cm (8 inch) cake tin with greased greaseproof paper. Turn the cake mixture into the tin and bake in a moderate oven (170°C, 325°F, gas mark 3) for one and a half hours until the cake is cooked. (A clean knife inserted into the cake should not show any trace of moist cake when withdrawn.)

GRANNY'S GINGERBREAD

METRIC
400 g plain flour
3 teaspoons baking powder
1 teaspoon bicarbonate of soda
3 teaspoons ground ginger
½ teaspoon salt
200 g demerara sugar
150 g butter
150 g treacle
150 g golden syrup
250 ml milk
1 egg

IMPERIAL
1 lb plain flour
3 teaspoons baking powder
1 teaspoon bicarbonate of soda
3 teaspoons ground ginger
½ teaspoon salt
8 oz demerara sugar
6 oz butter
6 oz treacle
6 oz golden syrup
½ pint milk
1 egg

Sift the flour, baking powder, bicarbonate of soda, ginger and salt together. Warm the sugar, butter, treacle and syrup together until the butter has just melted. Lightly beat the egg and add to the milk. Stir into the treacle mixture. Make a well in the centre of the flour and pour in the treacle mixture. Mix well. Line a greased 23 cm (9 inch) square tin with greased greaseproof paper. Turn the cake mixture into the tin. Bake in a moderate oven (170°C, 325°F, gas mark 3) for one and a half hours. Turn on to a wire tray and mark into 5 cm (2 inch) squares. Decorate each with whipped cream.

APPLE UPSIDE DOWN CAKE

METRIC
Fruit layer
200 g cooking apples
3 tablespoons caster sugar
25 g butter
Cake
50 g butter
50 g caster sugar
50 g self raising flour
1 egg
clotted cream

IMPERIAL
Fruit layer
8 oz cooking apples
3 tablespoons caster sugar
1 oz butter
Cake
2 oz butter
2 oz caster sugar
2 oz self raising flour
1 egg
clotted cream

Fruit layer: Peel and core the apples and cut into slices. Put in a pan and just cover with water. Bring to the boil to soften the fruit but keep the slices intact. Melt the butter in an 18 cm (7 inch) cake tin and coat the bottom of the tin. Lightly grease the sides of the tin. Sprinkle sugar over the butter. Carefully place the apple slices over the caramel mixture in the cake tin making an attractive pattern.

Cake: Cream the butter and sugar until light and fluffy. Beat the egg and beat into the creamed mixture. Fold in the flour. Spoon the cake mixture over the fruit. Bake in a moderate oven (180°C, 350°F, gas mark 4) for 30 minutes until the cake is cooked. Turn out with fruit side up. Serve with clotted cream.

SCONES

CORNISH SCONES

METRIC	IMPERIAL
200 g self raising flour	8 oz self raising flour
50 g butter	2 oz butter
25 g caster sugar	1 oz caster sugar
1 egg	1 egg
milk	milk
pinch of salt	pinch of salt
125 ml clotted cream	¼ pint clotted cream
strawberry jam	strawberry jam

Sift the flour and salt together. Rub the butter into the flour until the mixture looks like breadcrumbs. Stir in the sugar. Lightly beat the egg and add with enough milk to give a soft, light dough. Roll out on a floured board to a thickness of 1.5 cm (⅟ inch) and cut into 5 cm (2 inch) rounds. Bake on a lightly greased baking sheet in a hot oven (230ºC, 450ºF, gas mark 8) for 10 - 15 minutes until cooked. Serve with strawberry jam and clotted cream.

ICED SCONES

Make as for Cornish Scones but stir 1 tablespoon chopped glacé cherries into the flour mixture with the sugar and coat the cooked scones with glacé icing. Decorate each scone with half a cherry.

COUNTRY SCONES

Make as for Cornish Scones but stir 50 g (2 oz) mixed currants and sultanas into the flour mixture with the sugar.

GRIDDLE SCONES

Make as for Cornish Scones but cook on a hot, lightly greased griddle. Turn the scones after a few minutes to cook both sides.

CHEESE SCONES

METRIC	IMPERIAL
200 g self raising flour	*8 oz self raising flour*
50 g butter	*2 oz butter*
1 teaspoon baking powder	*1 teaspoon baking power*
100 g Cheddar cheese	*4 oz Cheddar cheese*
1 teaspoon mustard powder	*1 teaspoon mustard powder*
125 ml milk	*¼ pint milk*
pinch of salt	*pinch of salt*

Sift the flour, salt and baking powder together. Rub the butter into the flour until the mixture looks like breadcrumbs. Grate the cheese. Stir in the mustard and half the cheese. Add enough milk to give a soft, light dough. Roll out on a floured board to a thickness of 1.5 cm (½ inch) and cut into 5 cm (2 inch) rounds. Brush the tops with milk and sprinkle over the rest of the cheese. Bake on a lightly greased baking sheet in a hot oven (220ºC, 425ºF, gas mark 7) for 10 minutes until cooked.

DROP SCONES

METRIC	IMPERIAL
200 g self raising flour	8 oz self raising flour
50 g butter	2 oz butter
50 g caster sugar	2 oz caster sugar
1 egg	1 egg
125 ml milk	¼ pint milk
125 ml water	¼ pint water
pinch of salt	pinch of salt
fat for frying	fat for frying

Sift the flour and salt together. Rub the butter into the flour until the mixture looks like breadcrumbs. Stir in the caster sugar. Mix the water and milk together. Make a well in the centre of the flour mixture. Beat the egg and add with a little of the milk and water liquid. Beat until smooth. Add the rest of the liquid taking care that no lumps are formed. Leave to stand for 15 minutes in a cool place. Heat and lightly grease a griddle or thick frying pan. Drop spoonfuls of the scone mixture on to the griddle. Cook until bubbles form on the surface of the scones and then turn them to cook the other side. Serve hot with butter and raspberry or strawberry jam.

FRUIT DROP SCONES

Stir 50 g (2 oz) mixed fruit (sultanas and currants) into the mixture with the sugar.

SMALL CAKES AND BUNS

STRAWBERRY CUP CAKES

METRIC
200 g self raising flour
100 g butter
150 g caster sugar
2 eggs
125 ml milk
pinch of salt
cream
strawberries

IMPERIAL
8 oz self raising flour
4 oz butter
6 oz caster sugar
2 eggs
¼ pint milk
pinch of salt
cream
strawberries

Cream the butter and sugar until light and fluffy. Beat the eggs and beat into the creamed mixture a little at a time. Sift the flour and salt and fold into the creamed mixture alternately with the milk. Spoon into patty cases in a small cakes tin. Bake in a moderately hot oven (200ºC, 400ºF, gas mark 6) for 10 - 15 minutes until the cakes are cooked and have peaked. When cool, cut a slice from the top of each cake. Decorate the cakes with whipped cream and strawberries. Cut the removed cake slices in half and place on top of the cakes.

FRUIT BUNS

METRIC	IMPERIAL
200 g plain flour	*8 oz plain flour*
100 g butter	*4 oz butter*
100 g demerara sugar	*4 oz demerara sugar*
100 g dried mixed fruit	*4 oz dried mixed fruit*
2 teaspoons baking powder	*2 teaspoons baking powder*
1 teaspoon mixed spice	*1 teaspoon mixed spice*
grated rind of 1 lemon	*grated rind of 1 lemon*
1 egg	*1 egg*

Sift the flour, baking powder and mixed spice together. Rub the butter into the flour until the mixture looks like breadcrumbs. Stir in the lemon rind, sugar and fruit. Make a well in the middle of the cake mixture. Beat the egg and pour into the well. Mix to give a stiff, crumbly consistency. Add a little milk if necessary. Spoon in 12 small heaps on a greased baking sheet and bake in a moderately hot oven (200ºC, 400ºF, gas mark 6) for 15 - 20 minutes.

CHOCOLATE FINGERS

Whisk 1 egg with 3 tablespoons caster sugar until the mixture retains the impression of the whisk for a few seconds. Sift 2 tablespoons strong plain flour over the mixture and fold in lightly using a metal spoon. Fold in a further 2 tablespoons strong plain flour. Spoon the mixture into a piping bag with a 1 cm (1 inch) nozzle and pipe the mixture on to non-stick paper on a baking sheet. Bake in a moderately hot oven (200ºC, 400ºF, gas mark 6) for 8 - 10 minutes until golden. When cool, dip the ends of the fingers in melted chocolate.

RUM TRUFFLES

METRIC	IMPERIAL
50 g plain biscuits or cake	*2 oz plain biscuits or cake*
100 g plain chocolate	*4 oz plain chocolate*
50 g butter	*2 oz butter*
2 teaspoons caster sugar	*2 teaspoons caster sugar*
3 teaspoons rum or sherry	*3 teaspoons rum or sherry*
apricot jam	*apricot jam*
chocolate strands	*chocolate strands*
1 tablespoon double cream	*1 tablespoon double cream*

Melt the plain chocolate in a basin over a pan of hot but not boiling water. Remove from the heat and beat in the butter. Add the cream, sugar and rum. Crumble the biscuits or cake and beat into the chocolate mixture. Leave to stand until the mixture is firm. Shape into small balls. Coat each with jam and roll in chocolate strands.

COCONUT TRUFFLES

Coat the truffles with coconut instead of chocolate strands.

BATH BUNS

METRIC	IMPERIAL
400 g strong plain flour	*1 lb strong plain flour*
15 g fresh yeast or	*½ oz fresh yeast or*
* 7 g dried yeast and 1 teaspoon caster sugar*	* ¼ oz dried yeast and 1 teaspoon caster sugar*
125 ml tepid milk	*¼ pint tepid milk*
4 tablespoons tepid water	*4 tablespoons tepid water*
1 teaspoon salt	*1 teaspoon salt*
50 g butter	*2 oz butter*
50 g caster sugar	*2 oz caster sugar*
150 g sultanas	*6 oz sultanas*
3 tablespoons chopped peel	*3 tablespoons chopped peel*
2 eggs	*2 eggs*
1 egg and sugar lumps for coating	*1 egg and sugar lumps for coating*

If fresh yeast is used, blend it with half the tepid milk and water. (If dried yeast is used, dissolve the teaspoon of sugar in half the tepid milk and water and sprinkle the dried yeast on top of the liquid.) Leave the yeast mixture until frothy. Place a quarter of the flour in a bowl and add the yeast liquid and the remainder of the milk and water. Mix well. Leave in a warm place to rise for 20 minutes. Warm the butter but do not melt it. Sift the remaining flour and salt together and stir in the sugar. Lightly beat the eggs. Stir the butter and eggs into the yeast mixture. Add the flour and sugar mixture, sultanas and peel. Mix to a smooth dough. Turn on to a floured board and knead lightly. Leave in a covered bowl until it doubles in size. Knead lightly. Place in spoonfuls on a greased baking sheet leaving space for the mixture to rise. Roughly crush the sugar lumps. Brush the buns with lightly beaten egg and sprinkle with the broken sugar lumps. Bake in a moderately hot oven (190°C, 375°F, gas mark 5) for 15 minutes. Serve buttered.

DEVONSHIRE SPLITS

METRIC	IMPERIAL
15 g fresh yeast	*¼ oz fresh yeast*
or 7 g dried yeast and 1 teaspoon caster sugar	*or ¼ oz dried yeast and 1 teaspoon caster sugar*
250 ml tepid milk	*¼ pint tepid milk*
400 g strong plain flour	*1 lb strong plain flour*
50 g butter	*2 oz butter*
25 g sugar	*1 oz sugar*
1 teaspoon salt	*1 teaspoon salt*
cream	*cream*
jam	*jam*
icing sugar	*icing sugar*

If fresh yeast is used, blend it with half the milk. (If dried yeast is used, dissolve the teaspoonful of sugar in half the tepid milk and sprinkle the dried yeast on top of the liquid.) Leave the yeast mixture until frothy. Sift the flour and salt together. Make a well in the centre of the flour. Melt the butter and add with the sugar to the remaining milk. Pour this milk mixture and the yeast liquor into the centre of the flour. Work to an elastic dough, turn on to a floured board and knead until smooth. Cover with a cloth and leave in a warm place until the dough has risen to twice its size. Turn on to a lightly floured board and divide into 16 pieces. Knead each piece into a small ball and then flatten with the palm of the hand. Place on a greased baking sheet and leave to rise in a warm place for 20 minutes. Bake in a hot oven (220°C, 425°F, gas mark 7) for 15-20 minutes. To serve, split open and spread with jam and whipped cream. Sprinkle with icing sugar.

TEACAKES

METRIC
300 g plain flour
15 g fresh yeast or
  7 g dried yeast and 1 teaspoon caster sugar
200 ml tepid milk and water
25 g fat
1 egg
75 g sultanas and currants mixed
pinch of salt

IMPERIAL
12 oz plain flour
½ oz fresh yeast or
  ¼ oz dried yeast and 1 teaspoon caster sugar
⅓ pint tepid milk and water
1 oz fat
1 egg
3 oz sultanas and currants mixed
pinch of salt

Sift the flour. If fresh yeast is used, blend it with half the tepid milk and water. (If dried yeast is used, dissolve the teaspoon of sugar in half the tepid milk and water and sprinkle the dried yeast on top of the liquid.) Leave the yeast mixture until it is frothy. Add the rest of the liquid. Make a well in the centre of the flour and pour the yeast liquid into it. Lightly beat the egg and mix into the flour. Melt the fat and work into the flour mixture. Knead until the dough is smooth. Cover and leave in a warm place until the dough has doubled in size. Knead the salt and fruit into the dough. Form into 12 flat rounds and place on a greased baking sheet. Cover and leave to stand in a warm place for 15 minutes. Preheat the oven to 230°C, 450°F, gas mark 8. Bake the buns for 15 minutes. Turn on to a wire tray to cool. Serve split, buttered or toasted.

TARTS AND FLANS

STRAWBERRY JAM TART

METRIC
Shortcrust pastry
200 g plain flour
100 g butter
8 teaspoons water
pinch of salt
Filling
strawberry jam
cream

IMPERIAL
Shortcrust pastry
8 oz plain flour
4 oz butter
8 teaspoons water
pinch of salt
Filling
strawberry jam
cream

Pastry: Sift the flour and salt together. Rub in the fat until the mixture looks like breadcrumbs. Add the water and form into a lump.

Filling: Use half the pastry to line a 25 cm (10 inch) ovenproof plate. Spread generously with strawberry jam. Roll out the remainder of the pastry and cover the jam. Brush with milk and sprinkle lightly with sugar. Cook in a moderately hot oven (200°C, 400°F, gas mark 6) for 20 minutes until the pastry is cooked and lightly browned. Serve with cream.

RASPBERRY FRUIT TART

Make as for strawberry jam tart above but use 150 g (6 oz) fresh, washed raspberries instead of jam. Moisten with water and sweeten with sugar. When the tart is cooked, dust with caster sugar and serve with cream.

STRAWBERRY FLAN

METRIC	IMPERIAL
Shortcrust pastry	*Shortcrust pastry*
Filling	*Filling*
200 g strawberries	*8 oz strawberries*
¼ packet strawberry jelly	*¼ packet strawberry jelly*
cream	*cream*

Pastry: Make the pastry as on page 21. Line a 20 cm (8 inch) flat tin with the pastry. Prick the pastry all over with a fork and bake blind in a moderately hot oven (200°C, 400°F, gas mark 6) for 20 minutes.

Filling: Make the jelly following the instructions on the packet. (Only a quarter of the water is needed since only a quarter of the jelly is used.) Leave to cool. Wash and hull the strawberries. Place in the flan case, keeping a few for decoration. When the jelly has begun to set, pour over the fruit. Leave to set. Whip the cream and pipe rosettes around the edge of the flan and in the middle. Place the strawberries on top of the cream rosettes.

APPLE CRUMBLE

METRIC	IMPERIAL
400 g cooking apples	*1 lb cooking apples*
150 g self raising flour	*6 oz self raising flour*
75 g butter	*3 oz butter*
75 g demerara sugar	*3 oz demerara sugar*
cream	*cream*

Peel and core the apples. Slice and place in a saucepan with a very little cold water. Bring to the boil to soften the apples. Place in a pie dish. Rub the butter into the flour until the mixture looks like breadcrumbs. Stir in the sugar. Sprinkle over the fruit. Bake in a moderately hot oven (190°C, 375°F, gas mark 5) for 35 minutes. Serve with cream. Soft fruit such as raspberries, blackberries, gooseberries, or plums may be used instead of apples.

CHOCOLATE TART

METRIC	IMPERIAL
Shortcrust pastry	*Shortcrust pastry*
Filling	*Filling*
50 g self raising flour	2 oz self raising flour
50 g butter	2 oz butter
50 g caster sugar	2 oz caster sugar
25 g ground almonds	1 oz ground almonds
1 tablespoon cocoa	1 tablespoon cocoa
1 tablespoon raspberry jam	1 tablespoon raspberry jam
2 teaspoons finely grated lemon rind	2 teaspoons finely grated lemon rind
1 egg	1 egg
cream	cream

Pastry: Make the pastry as on page 21 using half the quantities. Line an 18 cm (7 inch) ovenproof flan dish.
Filling: Spread the jam over the pastry. Cream the butter and caster sugar. Lightly beat the egg and beat into the butter mixture. Sift the flour and cocoa together and fold into the butter mixture with the ground almonds and grated lemon rind. Turn the mixture into the pastry case and cover with strips of pastry. Bake in a moderately hot oven (200°C, 400°F, gas mark 6) for 15 minutes to set the pastry and then reduce the temperature to 180°C, 350°F, gas mark 4 for 15 minutes until the filling is cooked. Serve with whipped cream.

STRAWBERRY TARTS

METRIC
Pastry
Filling
200 g strawberries
Glaze
3 tablespoons sieved red jam
2 tablespoons water
1 tablespoon lemon juice
cream

IMPERIAL
Pastry
Filling
8 oz strawberries
Glaze
3 tablespoons sieved red jam
2 tablespoons water
1 tablespoon lemon juice
cream

Pastry: Make pastry as on page 21 and line small tartlet tins. Prick the bottoms and bake blind in a moderately hot oven (200°C, 400°F, gas mark 6) for 20 minutes until the pastry is cooked and lightly browned.

Glaze: Heat the jam, water and lemon juice over a low heat stirring until the glaze hangs in heavy drops from the spoon. Brush the pastry cases with the hot glaze.

Filling: Wash and hull the strawberries and fill the pastry cases. Brush the fruit with the glaze. Top with whipped cream.

[For white fruit such as apples use apricot jam in the glaze. If necessary poach the fruit first in a little syrup until it is tender. Brush apples and pears with a little lemon juice to stop them discolouring.]

TRIFLES AND CREAMS

STRAWBERRY TRIFLE

METRIC
Trifle
6 sponge cakes
strawberry jam
1 strawberry jelly
150 g strawberries
2 tablespoons sherry
250 ml cream
Custard
500 ml milk
⅟ vanilla pod
2 eggs and 2 egg yolks
2 tablespoons caster sugar

IMPERIAL
Trifle
6 sponge cakes
strawberry jam
1 strawberry jelly
6 oz strawberries
2 tablespoons sherry
⅟ pint cream
Custard
1 pint milk
⅟ vanilla pod
2 eggs and 2 egg yolks
2 tablespoons caster sugar

The trifle: Make the jelly, following the instructions on the side of the packet. Leave to cool. Split and jam the sponge cakes and place at the bottom of a glass trifle dish. Pour the sherry over the sponge cakes. Wash and hull the fruit. Place the fruit on top of the sponge cakes, keeping a few for decoration. Pour the jelly over the fruit and sponge cakes. When the jelly is set, pour the cooled custard on top. Leave to set. Whip the cream and pile on top of the trifle. Decorate with strawberrries.

Custard: Warm the milk with the vanilla pod until just boiling. Remove from the heat and leave to stand for 20 minutes. Remove the pod. Beat the eggs, egg yolks and sugar together and strain into the milk. Warm gently, stirring until the custard thickens slightly. Do not allow to boil. Sprinkle a little sugar over the surface (to stop a skin forming) and leave to cool.

APPLE AND CIDER TRIFLE

METRIC	IMPERIAL
Trifle	*Trifle*
6 sponge cakes	6 sponge cakes
1 kg dessert apples	2 lb dessert apples
1 lemon	1 lemon
100 g sugar	4 oz sugar
3 tablespoons cider	3 tablespoons cider
2 tablespoons brandy (optional)	2 tablespoons brandy (optional)
2 tablespoons raspberry jam	2 tablespoons raspberry jam
Syllabub	*Syllabub*
250 ml double cream	½ pint double cream
50 g caster sugar	2 oz caster sugar
125 ml cider	¼ pint cider
apple slices for decoration	apple slices for decoration

Trifle: Peel, core and slice the apples. Squeeze the lemon and grate the rind. Put the apple, sugar, lemon juice and rind in a saucepan and cook gently for 15 minutes until the apples are soft. Drain, leaving the apple juice and fruit to cool separately. Split and jam the sponge cakes and place at the bottom of a glass trifle dish. Spoon the fruit on top of the sponge cakes. Mix 8 tablespoons of the apple juice with the cider and brandy and spoon over the fruit and sponge cakes. Cover and place in the refrigerator for 1 hour.

Syllabub: Place the cream, caster sugar and cider in a bowl and whisk until thick. Pile on top of the trifle. Brush the apple slices with a little lemon juice to stop them discolouring and use to decorate the trifle.

STRAWBERRY CREAMS

METRIC	IMPERIAL
200 g strawberries	*8 oz strawberries*
50 g caster sugar	*2 oz caster sugar*
2 teaspoons lemon juice	*2 teaspoons lemon juice*
125 ml double cream	*¼ pint double cream*

Wash and hull the fruit. Purée the strawberries and stir in the lemon juice and caster sugar. Whip the cream and fold into the purée (keeping a little for decoration). Spoon into individual dishes and freeze. Decorate each dish with a rosette of cream topped with a strawberry.

RASPBERRY CREAMS

Use 200 g (8 oz) raspberries instead of strawberries in the recipe above. The raspberry purée should be sieved to remove the seeds.

STRAWBERRY SOUFFLÉ

METRIC	IMPERIAL
150 g strawberries	6 oz strawberries
75 g caster sugar	3 oz caster sugar
3 eggs	3 eggs
1 tablespoon powdered gelatine	1 tablespoon powdered gelatine
1 tablespoon lemon juice	1 tablespoon lemon juice
125 ml double cream	¼ pint double cream
125 ml single cream	¼ pint single cream

Wash and hull the strawberries. Sieve or liquidise the fruit keeping a few for decoration. Separate the egg yolks and whites. Warm the yolks, sugar and lemon juice with 1 tablespoon water in a bowl that is standing over hot water. Whisk until the mixture is thick. Remove from the heat and beat. Place the gelatine in a pan with 2 tablespoons warm water. Leave to soak for a few minutes and then stir over a low heat until the gelatine has dissolved. Pour into the egg mixture. Stir the egg mixture into the strawberry purée. Whip the creams together until thick. Beat the egg whites until stiff. Fold the cream and egg whites alternately into the strawberry mixture using a large metal spoon. Place a strip of greaseproof paper around the outside of a half litre (1 pint) soufflé dish so that the paper stands 5 cm (2 inches) above the rim of the dish. Secure the paper with an elastic band or paper clip. Spoon the fruit mixture into the dish and chill in the refrigerator until set. To serve, remove the paper collar and decorate the soufflé with strawberries.

RASPBERRY SOUFFLÉ

Use 150 g (6 oz) raspberries instead of the strawberries in the above recipe.

SAVOURIES

CHEESE AND POTATO PIE

METRIC
200 g potatoes
75 g Cheddar cheese
1 onion
25 g butter
4 tablespoons milk
4 eggs
salt and pepper
parsley

IMPERIAL
8 oz potatoes
3 oz Cheddar cheese
1 onion
1 oz butter
4 tablespoons milk
4 eggs
salt and pepper
parsley

Peel the potatoes and boil in salt water for 15 to 20 minutes until soft. Skin and chop the onion and fry in half the butter until softened but not discoloured. Grate the cheese. Drain the potatoes, season and mash with the remaining butter and the milk. Mix in the onion and two thirds of the cheese. Place in a heat proof dish. Make four small hollows in the surface of the potato mixture. *Crack each egg into a cup and gently place an egg in each hollow. Dot with butter. Sprinkle the remaining cheese over the pie. Bake in a moderately hot oven (190ºC, 375ºF, gas mark 5) for 15 minutes until the eggs are set. If the cheese on top has not browned, place the pie under a grill for a few minutes before serving. Garnish with parsley and serve with mixed salad.

[*Alternatively, poach the eggs and place an egg in each hollow. Dot with butter. Sprinkle the remaining cheese over the pie and place under a grill for a few minutes to brown the cheese.]

HAM WITH HONEY SAUCE

METRIC	IMPERIAL
1 kg leg of gammon ham	*2 lb leg of gammon ham*
Honey sauce	***Honey sauce***
2 tablespoons sugar	*2 tablespoons sugar*
4 tablespoons water	*4 tablespoons water*
2 tablespoons clear honey	*2 tablespoons clear honey*
2 tablespoons cornflour	*2 tablespoons cornflour*
4 tablespoons sherry	*4 tablespoons sherry*

Soak the ham in cold water for 12 hours. Remove from the water and steam for 2¼ - 2¼ hours until cooked. Cut into slices.

Honey sauce: Dissolve the sugar in the water in a saucepan and stir in the honey. Mix the cornflour with the sherry and stir into the honey mixture. Heat gently until boiling, stirring all the time until the sauce thickens. Pour over the gammon slices and leave over the steamer for 3 minutes. Serve with salad and brown bread.

WEST COUNTRY SAUSAGE

METRIC	IMPERIAL
400 g minced beef	*1 lb minced beef*
400 g minced ham	*1 lb minced ham*
150 g breadcrumbs	*6 oz breadcrumbs*
1 medium sized onion	*1 medium sized onion*
25 g butter	*1 oz butter*
¼ teaspoon grated nutmeg	*¼ teaspoon grated nutmeg*
¼ teaspoon ground mace	*¼ teaspoon ground mace*

METRIC	IMPERIAL
1 egg	*1 egg*
salt and pepper	*salt and pepper*
toasted breadcrumbs for coating	*toasted breadcrumbs for coating*

Skin and dice the onion. Fry in the butter until softened. Mix the meats together and stir in the breadcrumbs. Add the meats and seasonings to the pan. Beat the egg and use to bind the mixture together. Place in a damp cloth, tie and boil for three hours or turn into a loaf tin lined with greased greaseproof paper, cover with foil and bake at 150°C, 300°F, gas mark 2 for three and a half hours. Leave to cool. Turn out and coat with toasted breadcrumbs. Serve with green salad.

RAW TATTIE FRY

METRIC	IMPERIAL
200 g potatoes	*8 oz potatoes*
2 onions	*2 onions*
4 slices bacon	*4 slices bacon*
4 pork sausages	*4 pork sausages*
250 ml water	*¼ pint water*
salt and pepper	*salt and pepper*

Fry the bacon in a large frying pan. Remove the bacon and keep warm. Skin and slice the onions. Fry lightly. Peel and thinly slice the potatoes. Add to the pan and stir. Gently pour the water over the potatoes. Season. Cover and heat gently for 20 minutes until the potatoes are softened. Fry the sausages separately. Before serving, remove the lid and crisp the potatoes. Place the potatoes and onion in the centre of a dish and surround with the sausages and bacon. [If preferred, a little flour may be worked into the fat after the onions have been fried and a stock cube with browning may also be added to the water before the liquid is poured over the potatoes.]

FISHERMAN'S PIE

METRIC	IMEPRIAL
400 g cod fillets	1 lb cod fillets
100 g peeled shrimps	4 oz peeled shrimps
1 kg potatoes	2 lb potatoes
50 g butter	2 oz butter
125 ml milk	¼ pint milk
25 g plain flour	1 oz plain flour
2 tablespoons chopped parsley	2 tablespoons chopped parsley
50 g Cheddar cheese	2 oz Cheddar cheese
salt and pepper	salt and pepper
milk to cream the potatoes	milk to cream the potatoes

Peel and boil the potatoes in salted water. Drain. Add 3 tablespoons milk and half the butter. Cream the potatoes until fluffy. Wash the cod fillets and place in a saucepan or fish kettle. Cover with salted water and bring to the boil. Put a lid on the pan and leave the fish in the hot water for 5 minutes. Remove the fish, skin and flake the flesh taking care to remove the bones. Melt the rest of the butter and stir in the flour using a wooden spoon. Remove from the heat and stir in the milk and 125 ml (¼ pint) of the fish-water. Heat, stirring all the time to avoid lumps forming. Simmer for 3 minutes. Remove from the heat and stir in the flaked fish, shrimps and parsley. Season. Turn into an ovenproof dish. Pile the creamed potatoes on top. Grate the cheese and sprinkle over the pie. Bake in a moderately hot oven (200°C, 400°F, gas mark 6) for 30 minutes until the pie is heated through and the cheese is browned.

SHRIMP BOATS

METRIC	IMPERIAL
12 small, cooked vol-au-vent cases	*12 small, cooked vol-au-vent cases*
100 g frozen shrimps	*4 oz frozen shrimps*
125 ml milk	*¼ pint milk*
1 tablespoon cornflour	*1 tablespoon cornflour*
knob butter	*knob butter*
rind of 1 lemon	*rind of 1 lemon*
1 bay leaf	*1 bay leaf*
salt and pepper	*salt and pepper*

Blend the cornflour to a smooth paste with a little of the milk. Simmer the rest of the milk with the lemon rind and bay leaf for 5 minutes. Strain and bring to the boil. Pour on to the blended cornflour stirring all the time to prevent lumps forming. Return to the pan and cook gently for 1 - 2 minutes. Add the butter and season. Stir in the shrimps and pour into the vol-au-vent cases. Serve immediately.

POTTED PRAWNS

METRIC	IMPERIAL
200 g peeled prawns	*8 oz peeled prawns*
75 g butter	*3 oz butter*
2 teaspoons lemon juice	*2 teaspoons lemon juice*
4 teaspoons chopped parsley	*4 teaspoons chopped parsley*

Finely chop the prawns, keeping a few for garnish. Beat the prawns with half the butter and lemon juice. Spoon into small individual dishes. Melt the rest of the butter and use to seal the dishes. Garnish with whole prawns and parsley. Keep refrigerated. Serve with brown bread.

PANCAKES

SEAFOOD PANCAKES

METRIC
Batter
100 g plain flour
1 teaspoon baking powder
1 egg
125 ml milk
pinch of salt
fat for frying
Filling
300 g peeled, cooked prawns
2 tablespoons plain flour
1 small onion
1 bay leaf
25 g butter
125 ml milk
125 ml cream
3 tablespoons chopped parsley
salt and pepper

IMPERIAL
Batter
4 oz plain flour
1 teaspoon baking powder
1 egg
¼ pint milk
pinch of salt
fat for frying
Filling
12 oz peeled, cooked prawns
2 tablespoons plain flour
1 small onion
1 bay leaf
1 oz butter
¼ pint milk
¼ pint cream
3 tablespoons chopped parsley
salt and pepper

Pancakes: Sift the flour, baking powder and salt together. Make a well in the centre of the flour. Add the egg and a little of the milk. Beat until smooth. Gradually add the rest of the milk, beating to keep the mixture smooth and free from lumps. Leave to stand in a cool place for 15 minutes to soften the flour. Heat a little fat in a small frying pan until it is very hot. Pour a little batter into the pan, tilting the pan so that the batter spreads thinly over the bottom.

When the underside is cooked, turn the pancake and cook the other side. Cook the rest of the batter and keep the pancakes warm.

Filling: Skin and slice the onion. Add the onion and bay leaf to the milk and warm for a few minutes. Melt the butter in a saucepan and work in the flour. Remove from the heat. Strain the milk and stir into the flour. Heat gently for 1 minute, stirring until the sauce thickens. Away from the heat stir in the cream, prawns, and parsley. Season. Place each pancake in an individual ovenproof dish. Spoon filling on to each pancake and fold over. Cover with buttered foil and cook in a moderately hot oven (200°C, 400°F, gas mark 6) for15 minutes.

[Other fillings include cooked, flaked cod or haddock - cook the fish in the milk with the onion and bay leaf and remove the flesh.]

APPLE FRITTERS

METRIC	IMPERIAL
Batter	*Batter*
Fritters	*Fritters*
4 cooking apples	*4 cooking apples*
caster sugar	*caster sugar*
ground cinnamon	*ground cinnamon*
fat for frying	*fat for frying*
cream	*cream*

Batter: Make the batter as on page 34.

Fritters: Peel and core the apples and cut into rings. Dip in the batter and fry in very hot fat. Drain off excess fat in kitchen paper. Toss the fritters in caster sugar and dust with a little cinnamon. Serve with cream.

RUM FRITTERS

Soak the apple rings in a little lemon juice and rum before coating with the batter.

BREAD

COUNTRY BREAD

METRIC
15 g fresh yeast or
   7 g dried yeast and 1 teaspoon caster sugar
700 g strong plain flour
2 teaspoons salt
400 ml tepid water

IMPERIAL
½ oz fresh yeast or
   ¼ oz dried yeast and 1 teaspoon caster sugar
1 lb 12 oz strong plain flour
2 teaspoons salt
¾ pint tepid water

If using fresh yeast, blend it with the water. (If using dried yeast, dissolve the sugar in the water and sprinkle the dried yeast on top of the water.) Leave the yeast mixture to stand until frothy. Sift the flour and salt together. Make a well in the centre of the flour and pour in the yeast liquid. Work in the flour to make a firm dough. Turn on to a floured board and knead until the dough is firm. Place in a large, oiled polythene bag and leave to stand in a warm place until the dough has doubled in size, (about 2 hours in a warm room). Turn on to a floured board, flatten and then knead until firm. Divide in two, form each half into an oblong and place in a greased tin. Place the tins in a polythene bag and leave in a warm place until the dough reaches the top of the tins. Remove from the polythene bag and bake in the centre of a hot oven (230ºC, 450ºF, gas mark 8) for 30 - 40 minutes. When cooked, the loaves sound hollow when tapped. Turn out on a wire rack to cool.

MILK ROLLS

METRIC
Ingredients as for white bread above
50 g lard

IMPERIAL
Ingredients as for white bread above
2 oz lard

METRIC
use half milk and half water

IMPERIAL
use half milk and half water

Make the dough as on page 36 but rub the lard into the flour mixture and make the dough with milk and water. After the dough has risen for the first time, break into pieces about 50 g (2 oz) in weight and place on a greased baking sheet. Leave space for the dough to rise. Place the baking tin in a polythene bag and leave to rise until the rolls have doubled in size. Bake in the centre of a hot oven (230°C, 450°F, gas mark 8) for 15 - 20 minutes.

FRUIT LOAF

METRIC
300 g plain flour
½ teaspoon bicarbonate of soda
1 teaspoon baking powder
225 g sultanas
2 tablespoons demerara sugar
9 tablespoons malt extract
2 eggs
250 ml milk

IMPERIAL
12 oz plain flour
½ teaspoon bicarbonate of soda
1 teaspoon baking powder
9 oz sultanas
2 tablespoons demerara sugar
9 tablespoons malt extract
2 eggs
½ pint milk

Sift the flour, bicarbonate of soda and baking powder together. Stir in the sultanas. Slowly heat the demerara sugar and malt extract together. Do not allow to boil. Pour on to the dry ingredients. Beat the eggs. Add with the milk and beat well. Grease and line a 1.7 litre (3 pint) loaf tin. Turn the bread mixture into the tin. Grease a baking sheet. Place the baking sheet on top of the loaf tin with the greased side down. Put a weight on top. Bake in a cool oven (150°C, 300°F, gas mark 2) for one and a half hours. Turn out and cool on a wire rack. Wrap and keep for two days before eating. Serve sliced and buttered.

SANDWICHES

BROWN AND WHITE CHECK SANDWICHES

white bread
wholemeal bread
butter

Slice and butter the bread. Stack 6 slices alternately (white, brown, white . . .) with different fillings between the slices. Press firmly together. Cut the pile into 2.5 cm (1 inch) strips. Garnish with cress.

RIBBON SANDWICHES

white bread
wholemeal bread
butter

Start with 2 slices white bread and 2 slices wholemeal bread. Stack these alternately (light-dark, light-dark) with different fillings between each slice. Press stack firmly together and slice crusts from all sides. Just before serving, cut stack down into 0.5 cm (¼ inch) thick ribbon slices.

Savoury butters

Mix creamed butter with any of the following: anchovy paste, chopped capers, cheese, chopped chives, mashed hard boiled egg, grated green pepper, drained horseradish, tomato ketchup, lemon juice, mustard, chopped onions, chopped parsley, chopped, cooked prawns, salmon paste, sardine, watercress.

Fillings

cream cheese, chopped chives and spring onions
cucumber slices
meat spread
fish spread
tomato slices and cheese
sweet pickles and cheese
chopped hard boiled eggs
mashed sardine with a little chopped parsley and lemon juice
chopped cooked chicken with bread, butter and thyme stuffing
pork with sage and onion stuffing
poached salmon and cucumber slices
prawn and mayonnaise
Cheddar cheese, tomatoes and onion
ham and mustard
mixed salad
peanut butter
cream cheese with celery
smoked salmon
cream cheese with chopped capers
tuna with finely chopped spring onion
chopped cooked turkey, diced celery and sweet pickle
hard boiled egg and cress

BISCUITS

OATY BISCUITS

METRIC	IMPERIAL
100 g butter	*4 oz butter*
100 g rolled oats	*4 oz rolled oats*
100 g plain flour	*4 oz plain flour*
100 g sugar	*4 oz sugar*
2 tablespoons golden syrup	*2 tablespoons golden syrup*
2 teaspoons water	*2 teaspoons water*
1 teaspoon bicarbonate of soda	*1 teaspoon bicarbonate of soda*
pinch of salt	*pinch of salt*

Cream the butter and sugar. Mix the oats, flour and salt and rub lightly into the butter/sugar mixture. Heat the water and syrup in a saucepan. Stir in the bicarbonate of soda. Mix the syrup into the flour mixture. Divide into small balls. Bake on a baking sheet for 10 minutes in a moderately hot oven (190°C, 375°F, gas mark 5).

BUTTER WAFERS

METRIC	IMPERIAL
100 g butter	*4 oz butter*
75 g sugar	*3 oz sugar*
1 egg	*1 egg*
1 teaspoon vanilla essence	*1 teaspoon vanilla essence*
75 g plain flour	*3 oz plain flour*
pinch of salt	*pinch of salt*

Cream the butter and sugar. Beat in the egg and vanilla essence. Sift the flour and salt together and stir into the mixture. Drop teaspoonfuls of the mixture on to a greased baking sheet and bake in a moderately hot oven (190°C, 375°F, gas mark 5) for 10 minutes.

CHOCOLATE BUTTER WAFERS

Replace 2 tablespoons of the flour by 2 tablespoons cocoa.

SHORTBREAD FINGERS

METRIC	IMPERIAL
100 g butter	*4 oz butter*
50 g caster sugar	*2 oz caster sugar*
100 g plain flour	*4 oz plain flour*
50 g ground rice	*2 oz ground rice*
caster sugar to dredge	*caster sugar to dredge*

Cream the butter and sugar until light and fluffy. Stir in the flour and ground rice and bind the mixture together. Knead well to form a smooth dough. Roll out the dough on a floured board and cut into strips 5 cm by 2.5 cm (2 inches by 1 inch). Prick the surface using a fork and place the fingers on a greased baking sheet. Bake in a moderate oven (180°C, 350°F, gas mark 4) for 15 minutes until pale golden brown. Cool on a wire tray and dredge with caster sugar.

JAMS

STRAWBERRY JAM

METRIC	IMPERIAL
1 kg strawberries	*2 lb strawberries*
1.25 kg granulated sugar	*2 ½ lb granulated sugar*
2 tablespoons lemon juice	*2 tablespoons lemon juice*
knob of butter	*knob of butter*

Hull and wash the strawberries. Place in a preserving pan with the lemon juice and simmer gently for 20 minutes until the fruit is really soft. Remove the pan from the heat and stir in the sugar until it has dissolved. Add the knob of butter. Bring to the boil and boil rapidly for about 20 minutes until the setting point is reached. Take away from the heat and remove any scum from the surface of the jam. Leave to stand for 15 minutes then pot in sterilized jars and close. **Setting point:** Put a little of the jam on a cold saucer and leave to cool. Push a finger gently through it. If the surface wrinkles, setting point has been reached. **Remove the pan from the heat while doing the test so that the temperature does not rise too high.** The setting point is the temperature (approximately 105°C, 221°F) to which the fruit mixture must be heated so that the jam will set when it cools. The temperature varies slightly with different fruits and it is important to check if the setting point has been reached.

RASPBERRY JAM

METRIC	IMPERIAL
2 kg raspberries	*4 lb raspberries*
2 kg granulated sugar	*4 lb granulated sugar*
knob of butter	*knob of butter*

Wash the fruit and place in a preserving pan. Simmer the fruit gently in its own juice for 20 minutes until it is soft. Remove from the heat and stir in the sugar. Add the butter and boil rapidly for about 30 minutes. Test for setting point. (See page 42). Remove any scum from the surface. Leave to stand for about 15 minutes then pot in sterilized jars and close.

PLUM JAM

METRIC
3 kg plums
900 ml water
3 kg granulated sugar
knob of butter

IMPERIAL
6 lb plums
1 ½ pints water
6 lb granulated sugar
knob of butter

Wash the plums and place in a preserving pan with the water. Simmer gently for 30 minutes until the fruit is soft and the contents are well reduced. Remove the pan from the heat and stir in the sugar. Add the butter. Bring to the boil and boil rapidly for 10 - 15 minutes stirring from time to time. When setting point is reached (see page 42), remove from the heat. Using a slotted spoon, remove stones from the jam and scum from the surface. Leave to stand for 15 minutes then pot in sterilized jars and close.

PRESERVES

APPLE CHUTNEY

METRIC	IMPERIAL
1.5 kg cooking apples	*3 lb cooking apples*
1.5 kg onions	*3 lb onions*
500 g sultanas	*1 lb sultanas*
2 lemons	*2 lemons*
600 g demerara sugar	*1¼ lb demerara sugar*
600 ml malt vinegar	*1 pint malt vinegar*

Peel, core and dice the apples. Skin and dice the onions. Squeeze the juice and grate the rinds of the lemons. Place the apples, onions, sultanas, lemon juice and rind, sugar and vinegar in a preserving pan. Bring to the boil then simmer for 3 hours, stirring occasionally, until the mixture has thickened and there is no excess liquid. Place in sterilized jars and close using airtight tops that are resistant to vinegar.

TOMATO CHUTNEY

METRIC	IMPERIAL
2 kg red tomatoes	*4 lb red tomatoes*
200 g demerara sugar	*8 oz demerara sugar*
2 tablespoons mustard seeds	*2 tablespoons mustard seeds*
1 tablespoon whole allspice	*1 tablespoon whole allspice*
1 teaspoon cayenne pepper	*1 teaspoon cayenne pepper*
4 teaspoons salt	*4 teaspoons salt*
450 ml malt vinegar	*¾ pint malt vinegar*

Immerse the tomatoes in boiling water for a few minutes to loosen the skins. Remove the skins. Tie the mustard seeds and allspice in a piece of muslin. Place the tomatoes, mustard seeds, allspice and cayenne pepper in a preserving pan. Simmer gently for 45 minutes. Using a wooden spoon break down the tomatoes to a pulp. Add the sugar, salt and vinegar. Simmer for two and a half hours until no excess liquid remains and the mixture has thickened. Remove the muslin bag. Place the chutney in sterilized pots and close with airtight tops that are resistant to vinegar.

MIXED PICKLES

METRIC
2 kg mixed vegetables (cauliflower,
cucumber, small onions, green
or red peppers and French beans)
125 g salt
1.5 litres spiced vinegar

IMPERIAL
4 lb mixed vegetables (cauliflower,
cucumber, small onions, green
or red peppers and French beans)
5 oz salt
3 pints spiced vinegar

Wash the cauliflower and break into florets. Peel and dice the cucumber. Skin the onions. Seed and slice the peppers, top and tail and slice the beans. Place the vegetables in a large bowl, sprinkling salt between each layer. Cover with water and leave overnight. Next day, rinse the vegetables, drain and dry on kitchen paper. Pack the vegetables in sterilized jars, making sure that each jar has a selection of the vegetables. Fill with spiced vinegar. Close with airtight tops that are resistant to vinegar.

Spiced vinegar: *1 litre (2 pints) vinegar, 2 tablespoons blade mace, 1 tablespoon whole allspice, 1 tablespoon cloves, 2 cinnamon sticks, 6 black peppercorns, 1 small bay leaf.*

Place all the ingredients in a saucepan and bring to the boil. Leave to cool and to stand for about two hours. Strain the vinegar through a piece of muslin into a jug. Instead of the spices, 25 g (1 oz) pickling spice may be used. Instead of heating, the vinegar may be prepared in advance by leaving the spices to stand in the unheated vinegar for two months.

ICE CREAMS AND SORBETS

STRAWBERRY ICE CREAM

METRIC	IMPERIAL
400 g strawberries	*1 lb strawberries*
200 g granulated sugar	*8 oz granulated sugar*
1 tablespoon lemon juice	*1 tablespoon lemon juice*
¼ teaspoon salt	*¼ teaspoon salt*
1 teaspoon gelatine	*1 teaspoon gelatine*
1 tablespoon cold water	*1 tablespoon cold water*
250 ml milk	*½ pint milk*
250 ml cream	*½ pint cream*

Wash and hull the strawberries. Mash or liquidise to a purée. Add the sugar, lemon juice and salt. Mix well and leave to cool in the refrigerator which should be set to its coldest setting. Soften the gelatine in the water and add to the milk. Warm gently to dissolve the gelatine but do not boil. Cool and stir into the fruit purée. Beat the cream and fold into the fruit mixture. Turn into a metal tray and freeze in the compartment of a refrigerator. Serve with fresh strawberries.

CHOCOLATE ICE CREAM

METRIC	IMPERIAL
600 ml cream	*1 pint cream*
200 g sugar	*8 oz sugar*
2 teaspoons vanilla essence	*2 teaspoons vanilla essence*

METRIC	IMPERIAL
pinch of salt	*pinch of salt*
50 g plain chocolate	*2 oz plain chocolate*
2 tablespoons hot water	*2 tablespoons hot water*

Scald the cream. Add the sugar and stir until dissolved. Add the salt and vanilla essence. Melt the chocolate and dissolve in the hot water. Stir into the mixture. Cool and freeze.

LEMON SORBET

METRIC	IMPERIAL
200 g sugar	*8 oz sugar*
4 lemons	*4 lemons*
2 egg whites	*2 egg whites*
600 ml water	*1 pint water*

Squeeze the lemons and grate the rinds. Dissolve the sugar in the water and boil for 2 minutes. Remove from the heat and add the lemon rinds. Cover and leave to stand for 10 minutes. When cool, add the lemon juice. Strain into a shallow freezer container. Freeze for 2 hours until mushy. Whisk the egg whites until stiff. Turn the mixture into a bowl and fold in the egg whites. Replace in the container and freeze until firm.

STRAWBERRY SORBET

Replace the lemons in the above recipe by 1 kg (2 lb) strawberries washed and hulled. Purée the fruit. Dissolve the sugar in 250 ml ($\frac{1}{4}$ pint) water and heat until syrupy. Stir into the strawberry purée with 1 tablespoon lemon juice. Cool. Pour the mixture into a shallow freezer and freeze for 3 - 4 hours until mushy. Whisk the egg whites until stiff. Turn the purée into a bowl and fold the egg whites into it. Return to the freezer container and freeze until firm.

INDEX